[handwritten: Claim the INCREASE!]

99 Questions
You must ask a Man
Before Sleeping with him
&
Definitely
Before Having

Sex

[handwritten: To: Isa Thanks in advance for all of your support! May you be blessed beyond measure! ♡ Armani ☺]

By
Armani Valentino

[handwritten signature: Armani]

Foreword by Big Boom

<u>Suggested Retail Price: $15.00</u>
To order books, schedule book signing, or speaking engagement call:

972.781.8404

www.armanivalentino.com

www.myspace.com/armanivalentino

Cover design by:
Cheryl Jones & Armani Valentino

Cover Graphics by:
Cheryl Jones
www.myspace.com/cjae1202

Art Direction by:
Armani Valentino

ISBN 13: 978-0-615-17654-1

Table of Contents

To whom it may concern:

It is my esteemed pleasure to be submitting this wonderful work to you. I pray that this letter reaches you in the best of health and spirits. At a young age, I had the opportunity to experience many hardships, difficulty, pain, and setbacks; However, I now understand that all great men and women have experienced many of the same trials and so much more.

There's this young lady I recently met. She says she really likes me. I don't know why, but she really does. During the process of getting to know her, I now understand why so many women have had such a hard time with men. The bottom line is, they don't ask enough questions, and if they do, they don't ask the right ones. Hence my book, 99 *Questions that You Must Ask a Man Before Sleeping with Him, and Definitely Before Having Sex.*

With the divorce rate in our country being extremely high, and the number of unmarried individuals, especially black women, it is not hard to see that there are underlying issues. There was a time when not too many people in America lived above their means. Now-a-days many women are more concerned about asking men questions about the kind of car they drive, and what corporation they work for, instead of getting to know his heart. I've known women that if they had not heard of the company, would simply move on to the next man. Although finances are important, there are many more questions that need to be asked.

I hope that this book will be used as a basic guide in helping women choose a decent man.

Sincerely,
Your Brother
Armani

Dedication

Thanks Mom!

This book is dedicated to you. It is also dedicated to your mother and your late grandmother (my great grandmother). I can count the number of men that I have seen each of you with. Of course you know Great Grandma was with Great Grandpa happily for nearly 65 years until they both passed. So, that's why I thank you and my grandmothers because they taught you. You are a virtuous woman! It's also dedicated to any woman in the world that truly wants to be a virtuous woman as Proverbs chapter 31 describes.

FOREWORD
by BIG BOOM

For years I have watched women try to understand men. It wasn't until I was in my fifties that I decided to help women understand us. In my book, "If You Want Closure in Your Relationships Start with Your Legs," I address the importance of asking questions. Many times, a woman will get involved with a man and has not addressed enough subjects to make an intelligent decision. Women don't ask enough of the right questions.

When introduced to Armani Valentino by a mutual friend, I was surprised that at such a young age, he was giving women ammunition to find, keep, and attract the right man into their life. He was basically giving them "The Game." He is right on point.

Most men are not going to volunteer information. In chapter 2 of his book, "The art of Asking Questions," I enjoy the way he tells the woman that she has to become an "Interview Expert." Then in chapter 4 when he addresses the issue of "Love & Sex and how to tell the difference," he touches some key issues women need to know. Women can easily become emotionally attached to a man that they have been intimate with. Therefore, the questions and advice that he gives should help address things that usually aren't addressed before having sex or getting emotionally involved with someone.

Armani Valentino is on time. His generation and others need this book. He talks straight words and gives great advice on many areas throughout the book.

Big Boom
Essence Best-Selling Author
"If You Want Closure in Your Relationship Start With Your Legs"

"My Heart"

From the poetry book, "The Perfect Girl"

Any man can risk his life,

But it takes a real man to risk his heart!

I'm putting my heart on the line for you.

Please tell me I can play the part.

You know I won't mistreat you.

So with me, you're not taking a chance.

But if a chance is what you think you need,

You can choose another man.

Just remember...He's gonna mess up.

As a matter-of-fact, they all will.

'Cause the love they say they have for you

You'll see for yourself that it's not real.

This woman once told me

That I was blessed to know whom I love,

And that the woman who was loved by me

Was even more blessed to be loved.

But then the man that was with her said,

"Yeah that's true, "

"But what really makes you blessed

Is when you know she loves you too."

Chapter 1
The Importance of Asking Questions

One of my favorite recording artists, Lauryn Hill, said on her "Miseducation of Lauryn Hill" album, "If you're looking for the answers, you have to ask the questions!"

This is an understatement when it comes to relationships of any kind, especially with those that may affect the heart. Many women seem to be so desperate to get a man, they don't invest the time to prepare questions to ask a man before sleeping with him. Many of you may be saying, "Well it's wrong to have sex before marriage anyway!" I agree with you totally. I don't know any religious belief that condones sex before marriage, also know as FORNICATION.

Conversely, if so many women in America are single and want a God-fearing man, are they really "Virtuous Women?" I am no one's judge, but I definitely know that the "Virtuous Woman" in the Bible (Proverbs 31) is not the picture of many of the women that I see today in every city that I have traveled. Chapter 14 goes into further detail about this topic.

Starting a new relationship with someone that you may feel is compatible with you is like going to court. This is why people years ago would ask, "Are you courting him/her?" When you go to court to plead your case, you are asked and ask questions to prove your innocence or guilt. During this process, you get to prove your case. In order to prove your case you bring in witnesses, evidence, professionals, etc. This used to be the common practice between males and females wanting to be in a relationship. What happened? When was the last time you asked a man why he and his last girlfriend, fiancé, or wife broke up?

Do you think you can change him that much? I figured out that most so-called grown folks are going to do what they want to do. When was the last time you asked a man if he had a girlfriend or a wife? It amazes me how many women don't even ask a man if has a girlfriend or wife. I don't feel sorry for women that are that desperate that they can't remember to ask a man that question. Do you really want a good man if you can't ask something that simple? I would have to say, "Emphatically no!"

Are you that desperate for a man? Do you need sex that bad? Do you need to be in love that badly that you can't love yourself enough to ask a couple of questions? Do you think you will run him away by asking a couple of questions? Well, if you ask him a few questions and he runs away, more than likely he is not the man for you.

I have female friends that meet a man and know that he isn't right for them. These same individuals will continue to date him anyway. How do you knowingly talk to a man that doesn't mean you any good at all? Is it because you think you are that much different than the last woman he was just involved with?

Have you ever taken a test that didn't have at least one question on it? I can't remember one in all the twenty or more years of test-taking that didn't in some way ask a question. I found that on every test that I was not prepared for, I failed!

Do you want to fail the test of finding a decent man? Well, it's definitely a test for you. Then, when you find one, will you be "Virtuous" enough to keep him?

Your SEX will not keep him. Your BOOTY will not keep him. Your BREAST will not keep him. Your THIGHS will not keep him. Your EYES will not keep him. Really in truly, you can't keep something that doesn't want to be kept.

What makes you different from the rest of the women? I was out one night promoting my group's CD and a beautiful young lady passed by that had a nice booty. An associate of mine, that is a great promoter, was like "Man do you see that." I asked him, "Do you know how many women have a booty?" He thought about it and said, "All of them!"

That question was enough for him to know that I was more concerned about selling my group's CD than seeing some woman's booty that every other man was gawking at. Although a woman's shape is naturally appealing to a man, it can only do so much and go so far.

I bet you are wondering what will keep a good man? Your VIRTUE! Your "Virtue" will make a good man into a GREAT MAN. At least that was my understanding when I read Proverbs 31. Asking enough of the right questions will get you the answers that will let you know whether or not a man is a good mate for you. The right questions may also lead you to ask yourself a few questions about whether or not you really are a "VIRTUOUS WOMAN."

**"If you're looking for the answers,
you have to ask the questions."**
-From Lauryn Hill's "Miseducation of Lauryn Hill" album-

Chapter 2
The Art of Asking Questions

Most men don't like being questioned by a woman. Therefore, mastering the art of asking a man questions should be very beneficial in extracting the information from him that you need to make a good choice. If you observe the male, even as a child you may notice a his evasive answers or hesitance to questions asked by the female gender.

The female, usually being the smarter of the two, knowingly or unknowingly, has an advantage when it comes to getting what they want. However, for most people, knowing what they want and knowing what they need seems to pose a problem.

Once again, let me reference another one of Lauryn Hill's songs, *When It Hurts So Bad*. Some of the lyrics are: *What you want might make you cry. What you need might pass you by...If you don't catch it. And what you need ironically will turn out what you want to be if you just let it.*. Start wanting what you need. If you don't already have her album get one from somewhere. She gives many people, especially women, great advice about relationships.

Who? What? When? Where? Why? How? These are all questions that you need to know in order to find the answers to your questions. Anyone who's ever taken a science course can also use the scientific method to figure out if the man is right for you.

When you're asking a man questions that you have interest in being in a relationship with, it's like a job interview. The interviewer will ask you questions about yourself that make you want to answer them because they're about you. People love to talk about their good qualities. By first asking you some questions you want to answer, interviewers are able to get answers from you to some trap questions.

Many people don't like to answer trap questions because trap questions are meant to expose your flaws or weaknesses. A lead in question helps to link questions together, usually in chronological order. It is asked before a trap question or a closing question.

Most jobs that I feel are worth getting, have more than one interview. In order to get to the next step in the interview process, you have to close the interview by asking the interviewer lead in questions before you're closing questions. **You must become an interview expert when it comes to choosing a good man.** You should look at a man that says he's interested in you as basically submitting an application to become your life partner.

Most jobs that are very easy to get usually have a high turn over rate, don't pay that well, and are usually a headache to deal with. It's also a job that most people don't want. A man and/or a woman can be this same way.

A man that knows how to answer trap questions, and make them sound good to your ears, isn't necessarily a good choice. Once a man finds out what you want or like, he's going to try and conform to you. He may be seeing another woman and knows how she is and what she likes. However, he will conform to her when he is around her and conform to you when he is with you. Just as there is an art of asking questions, there is also an art of answering questions.

In the latter part of the book, you will notice that many of the questions are stated in different ways, but may mean the same thing. It is important that you ask the same questions different ways at different times. If the answers don't add up to be the same when the question is asked at a different time, he is more than likely not telling the truth.

The following are a couple of examples of lead in and trap questions:

What would you say your biggest weakness was? (trap)

They would lead you into this question with a lead in question such as:

What would you say your biggest strength is?

Now by asking this it gets you ready to answer the opposite question. Another example:

Out of all the positions here on your resume, which boss did you like the most and why? (lead in question)

Following that would more than likely be the trap question which is:

Which boss did you not get along with that well or which boss did you not like and why?

Therefore, this same process of asking questions may need to be taken when it comes to questioning a man that has interest in being with you. Remember this, people love to talk about themselves. LOL

**Learn to ask questions the right way,
but be sure to also watch and pray.**

-Armani Valentino-

Chapter 3
The 9 Most Important Questions to Ask

Now ladies, let's get down to what you've all been waiting for, the questions that you need to ask. The 9 questions in this chapter are what you absolutely must ask before sleeping with a man or having sex. Please make sure you read the previous chapters before reading anything else in this book. Make sure that you finish the book before you walk up to a man and ask him these questions. The last chapter of the book will let you know if you're ready to start asking a man the questions that will follow. Do not ask all 99 questions in this book at the same time. Please stay patient. The answers that you need will eventually be revealed.

Question #1: Are you Married? or *Do you have a girl-friend?* Also can be asked...Are you dating anyone else? Are you seeing anyone else? Are you sleeping with anyone else? Do you have any female friends that you're sleeping with, but you consider them to be just a friend? Are you on the down low? Please do not think that you can make a man stop seeing his female friends if he's not ready for that. But I guarantee you that by asking these questions throughout the book, you may EVENTUALLY factor out the other women.

Remember, have patience. Don't give yourself to him so soon. It's not a matter of fact of making him wait. It's for you. It's the whole process of respect, honor, and growing in love instead of falling in love. Too many women fall in love quickly and don't take the time to get to know the man.

These questions are to help protect your heart!

Question #2: Do you still go out with your Ex? <u>Can also be asked, Are you and your ex still seeing each other? Are you still having sex with your ex? When was the last time you had sex with your ex? Would you still have sex with your ex if she wanted to?</u> If this is the case, and the answer is "yes" to any of these questions, you may need to back up. You need to play it safe. She definitely has an advantage over you. She may not be as pretty as you, as smart, as funny, or as whatever than you are. However, they do have a history together. Especially if they were together for more than a year. Respect her and yourself since you're both women by allowing him the opportunity to get her emotionally out of his system. I'm not saying stop talking to him, but stick around just long enough to see whether or not it's a wise decision to continue getting to know him.

Question #3: Do you have children? Or <u>Do you want to have children?</u> Many women reading this may already have children or at least want to have children. If you don't ask, he may not tell you he has children. *Most men think that if you don't ask, and they don't tell, they didn't lie.* If he has children, find out how many? If he has more than one, find out if they are by more than one woman. You need to know if he's involved in the children's lives. If so, how much and how often. This may affect how much time you get to spend alone with him. It should also give you an idea of how he will treat your children if you have any. This may also affect your household budget in the future. If a man has multiple children (two or more) not by the same woman, and he's with neither of them, you could end up being next really quick.

Question #4: How often do you talk to your mom? I've found it to be rather true most of the time, that if a man doesn't have a good relationship with his mother he may not have good relationships with other women, particularly his mate. It is very important to learn how he relates to his mother and other female family members because this is more than likely how he will relate to you. You also need to know the values that his mother has taught him. His mother may not be living, and if not, ask him questions that may reveal the kind of relationship they shared.

Question #5: What kind of relationship are you looking for? A woman is often told by a man that he is not looking for anything serious, and she acts as if she did not hear him. Then, when she goes over his house unannounced and there is another female at his place or she sees him out in public holding hands with another female, she gets upset. He already told you what he was going to do by telling you that he did not want anything serious. Don't tell him that you are okay with that if you know that you are looking for something serious. Men usually tell the truth when it comes to this. Don't lie to yourself! Listen to what a man is telling you when he speaks on this subject. Don't think you can change him!

Question #6: <u>What type of relationship do you have with your father?</u> I didn't grow up with my father in the home, which for me was good because the type of man he was at that time. I remember being two years old, the name of the woman, and what she looked like, that my father was cheating on my mother with. I also remember how much stress and anguish this caused my mother.

As a young man raised in America, the absence of my father had a huge impact on how I treat women both positively and negatively. Especially, since I remember when he left!

Please get to know what type of relationship he had with his father. Even if his father was around, that may not be a good thing because the relationship that he saw his mother and father have may not have been a healthy one. He could have been molested, abused verbally or physically, or not shown any kind of love or attention from his father. In some cases, this is worse than the father being absent! It can leave very painful scars, and make him feel that he needs to gain power through treating his female partner in the same manner. It may also make him look at his money, cars, and other toys (women being one of them) as the definition of who he is. This will usually be shown when a man talks more about what he has during his conversation instead of who he is.

Question #7: Do you attend a regular spiritual service? Also can be asked as: <u>Do you have a relationship w/ God (Allah, Jehovah, Yahweh, or whatever name he or you may choose to call the Creator of the Heavens and the Earth)?</u>

Many people talk about being equally yoked. Many say that you should not marry anyone that doesn't attend the same church or is of a different religion than you. However, many people that were of the same religion have not had good relationships, but were supposed to be equally yoked. Two people making a decision to marry solely based on the religion of their preference may make certain things easier, but it doesn't ensure relationship success.

The Bible says that..."God is Love." In mathematics, "is" and "equal" mean the same thing. So, God = Love. If two people really love each other, feel that they are compatible, and both have a relationship with the Creator; it may be best to let nature take its course instead of interjecting just because they attend different churches or have different ideologies.

Some of you may be wondering why I saved this question to be number 7. Well, I was taught that the number 7 represents Spirituality or God. Others say that it is the number of completion, and I can understand because God is completion. However, there are only 9 numbers in Mathematics...1-9, and 0 is a place holder or is said to have no value. The number 9 being the last number would have to represent completion.

The number 9 is the only number that can be multiplied by any of the numbers, and still equal to be 9 when the numbers are all added up to equal a single digit. Here is another point to prove the number 9 is the number of completion: Erykah Badu, another one of my favorite recording artists, who was also one of the first 100 people to purchase a copy of this book, said on her first album, "I was born on the water with three dollars and six dimes. Yeah you may laugh cause you did not do your math." On her album, I believe she gave her meaning of this, of which I agree.

Now, let's further prove the number 9 represents completion. When a baby is conceived in the womb, it begins to grow and develop. This process usually takes an estimated period of 9 months to complete. The baby makes a half circle of 180 degrees before birth: 1+8+0 = 9. So, here you have 3 dollars and six dimes, which equals 360 pennies. Each penny represents a degree. 360 degrees makes a complete circle: 3+6+0 = 9. You have water, which is essential to all LIFE. Then, you have BIRTH. She was born into a Universe that has 9 known planets, of which water is on each of these. In a body that is made up of 9 major systems, each of which needs water to help sustain life. I think I'll stop here. Go get her albums, she gives great knowledge about relationships and life.

Question #8: When were you last tested for HIV?
This is a touchy subject. However, you must ask it to protect yourself. HIV/AIDS is one of the leading causes of death for women. This is a question that really needs to be asked before you even kiss a man. You also need to be tested yourself. If you know you have HIV/AIDS or any other STD, respect yourself and the man enough to let him know. Today some artists in music, television, film, and entertainment, are making works of art that are about being sexually involved with an individual. Not only are these works of art about being involved with one individual, but many are about being promiscuous. This causes the lower desires of the society to be enticed on a daily basis. What goes in the mind consciously or subconsciously is what is usually acted upon. Through this cycle of what I will call "Sex Marketing," individuals natural sex desires are heightened. Therefore, many men, and now women never seem to be satisfied with one individual. Once these desires are acted upon, relationships can be destroyed, families can be broken up, and lives can be lost. Children can also come into the world at a disadvantage because one question about being tested for STDs was never asked, nor answered.

The desire for sex is already strong in young males and females that seeing and hearing about it everywhere doesn't help one bit! Even young entrepreneurs see that selling sex can be rather profitable. However, once you become conscious of this, you also figure out that there are many other ways to make money. You may also learn to use the "Energy of Sex" to your advantage. I will speak more on this in chapters 4 and 41/2. So, be sure that you ask a man "When was the last time you were tested for HIV/AIDS?" If he is really serious about you, when the time comes for you to be sexually involved with the man, he should agree to go and get tested with you.

Ask him to go with you and get tested for STDs.

Question #9: How do you take care of yourself? <u>Do you work?</u> Basically, <u>Do you have a JOB?</u> If a man can work from home, has an independent business, is a food server, a janitor, a trash man, or CEO, it really shouldn't matter. As long as he is making money ethically, and striving to do better, this shouldn't be an issue. This seems to be the first question that is asked, but I feel that it shouldn't be. You shouldn't ask this first because you may miss out on a really good man by judging him by the kind of job he has. My mom is a certified school teacher and seriously doesn't make that much money. If a man is teaching school and doesn't make that much money, does that make him unqualified to be with you? Just because he is not making six figures or more a year is he unqualified to be with you? I feel people that choose to become teachers are very special individuals. They have really good hearts., and good benefits and retirement programs. LOL :-)

If you and a man are making only $25k—$30k a year each, you can live well. If you are really striving to be a virtuous woman according to Proverbs 31, you will understand that just as the virtuous woman made money and helped her husband, you should desire to do the same. Always have a desire to contribute.

There was a young lady I worked with at Victoria's Secret. She was very nice and attractive. She thought the same about me. One day, one of the women asked her and me had we thought about going out? Of course I had, and found out that she thought it was a great idea. When I asked about her friends that she usually went out with, she told me, "They're all married and their husbands go out with them." I thought this was great and looked forward to going out! I told her that at most I could pay for us to eat $50 each. She said, "I might as well pay for my own because where we usually eat the tab is about $80 per person." Now, let me remind you that I had just recently moved to Dallas, Texas, and was working 2 JOBS and my music business part-time. So to even spend $100 on a food date, I thought was great! Since we already knew each other from work I felt that we would have made a pretty good match. However, when she said that, I told her, "Well, looks like we won't be going out."

On a first date, or any date that you take a woman on, that is not your wife or committed life partner, you shouldn't have to spend over $100. Some of my most fun dates were $50 or less. Believe me I have had numerous dates that were much less than that. :-)

Maybe when I get the opportunity to come speak to you in your city, I will be able to share some of these stories about my most fun dates. I have known men and women that their money was all they were about, and didn't know how to have fun unless is cost them a lot of money.

Make sure that he is doing something productive. If a man has all the qualities hat you desire and genuinely wants to be with you, would you choose not be with because he doesn't make enough money? Are you seriously going to trade all of that for a man who may not have all of the qualities of this man, but makes more money? If you do, something has to be wrong with you!!!

I can hardly wait to share Chapter 14.

Ask me no questions, I'll tell you no lies.

-Unknown-

Note: It's Wednesday, November 22, 2006, at 3:40am. The funny part about this is, I haven't even written Chapter 14, but have it in my mind. I am really excited, so let me get to the next chapter in the book! Please, take your time when reading this book and don't just read it once. I advise reading it 5 times. Please write notes in it, underline certain points to remember, & talk about it with your girls.

Chapter 4 & 4 1/2

"Love & Sex"- How not to get the two confused

Love and Sex are the two most powerful energies in the Universe. Another music artist, actually a group called, "The Black-eyed Peas" said in a song, "You'll never know life if you never know love." I totally agree. Earlier, I mentioned that the Bible says, "God is Love." Well, Life is Love as well. So, Life = Love. You may be asking, "How is that?" If the original God is the Creator of Life, he would also be Life itself. Since we were made in his image and after his likeness, we are LIFE. He also created a way to produce and reproduce LIFE. We refer to this as SEX. Through the emotion of LOVE and the action of SEX, the best LIFE is created. Life can be created without love, but would it really be the best life that could be created? This is the reason why it is very easy to get the two confused.

Women, usually being the more emotional of the two sexes, seem to get this confused even more than men. This may be one of the reasons why every religion I know of is against FORNICATION. The Creator of the Heavens and Earth had to know this! If I never learned anything at all from one of my high school English teachers, I learned this:

One day in class, my English teacher was talking to us about some things and I could tell that something was wrong with her. Some of my classmates begin to ask questions about what was wrong and she didn't really want to tell what was wrong with her. However, she did leave this in my head when she said,

"Never date someone you wouldn't marry.
You just might fall in love with them."

Her words have stayed with me ever since. I thank her for that because many of you reading this book may be able to benefit from those words. She must have learned this the hard way because at such a late age in her life, I could tell she had some self-esteem problems possibly from the relationship she was in.

Writing that last sentence led my mind to say this to you as well, **"Every man is not marriage material."** Some of you may need to accept this.

I absolutely love the experience working for Victoria's Secret because about 95% of the time I was around women. I would observe, listen, and ask questions after and during work to my co-workers and sometimes customers about prior relationships. I heard many stories from many of the women at work that all seemed to have had a serious relationship that was really good, and they just decided one day that "they wanted to see what else was out there." This was one of the main reasons I heard from the women that had decent men that wanted to commit.

They talked about having a man that was doing them wrong or had done them wrong, and I would ask the question, "Well how did you get with this guy?" Most of them would say something like, "Well, I always thought he was cute, and finally said something to him. Thought he would be a better challenge than the guy I was with. The guy I was with was too nice, and I wanted a guy that was just a little more rough."

I couldn't believe the answers I received. I found out that most of them had at least one good man, but they took him for granted. After the other guy that they fell in lust with more than likely did them wrong, they were left standing there alone; Usually saying, "There aren't any good men out there!"

Sex is another subject I heard women talk about while working at Victoria's Secret. They would talk about sex not being good with an individual, or just felt that they could find better. Sexually speaking, others said "I just wanted to see what else was out there." Is a little sex worth losing a really good man? Most women that I spoke to said that when they did see what else was out there that it wasn't all that they thought it was going to be! Sex is an action! LOVE is an emotion! Sex is best experienced when two people both love and commit to one another as life partners. All the more reason the platform for marriage was created. In this type of environment LIFE can be created in LOVE.

Review Questions

1.) If you're looking for the answers, you have to ask the _____.

2.) You must become an _____ _____, when it comes to choosing a good man.

3.) Why do you feel it is important to ask questions?

_____
_____
_____
_____
_____
_____
_____
_____.

4.) The number 9 represents _____.

5.) Make up your own lead in question and write it below:

_____

_____

_____

_____

_____.

6.) Make up your own trap question and write it below:

_____

_____

_____

_____.

7.) _____ and _____ are the two most powerful energies in the _____.

8.) Never date someone you wouldn't marry because _____.

9.) Every man is not _____ _____.

Chapter 5

9 Spiritual Questions that you must ask

Spiritual not religious is what I mean. The differences in most religions that I have studied are very small. The differences are usually in the wording. If I call the Creator of the Heavens and Earth Jehovah and you call him Allah, God, Yahweh, The Great I am, or any other name you refer to the Creator, does that make me wrong? Does it make you right? Hmm... Just because someone attends a church, a mosque, a synagogue, or religious organization, doesn't mean they understand they are spiritual beings in physical bodies. I have found that many people don't know what they believe. They can say during a conversation what they don't believe, but don't know what they do believe. So, the following questions deal more with the spiritual development and how grounded in the Spirit of Spiritually an individual is.

Question #1: Do you believe that there is a Creator of the Heavens and the Earth? Can also be asked: Do you believe in God? This must be asked if you believe in the Creator. I wouldn't advise you continuing on with a man if he doesn't believe in the Creator.

Question #2: **Do you attend a spiritual meeting on a regular basis?** A commitment to spiritual development will usually transfer over to commitment to other areas of life. A man committed to developing his spiritual well-being will more than likely be committed to developing a relationship with a good woman.

Question #3: **Do you pray on a daily basis?** Prayer is better than sleep. In the early morning prayer that Muslims pray, there is a call to prayer.

In this call to prayer there is a part that says; Come to Prayer, Come to Success. Then, Prayer is better than sleep. When a man is under pressure and feels like he can't make it, he should call on the Creator. If he is the type of man that can call on God even before then, you may want to be with this type of man. If you already have someone like this you may want to hold on to him. He usually has developed a relationship with the Creator and understands the power that God has given him to change his situation. Man, this is a statement for myself at this point in my life!

Question #4: Does he study the scriptures on a regular basis? Whether this be the Bible, the Koran, the Torah, any other spiritual book, or even personal development and self-help books, each of them are based on the principles which improve an individual in the spiritual realm. The Bible says we're transformed through the renewing of the mind. In order to change the spiritual man/woman, there must be knowledge given to the brain that will enhance and renew the mind.

Question #5: What do you believe? This may be an issue that will be discussed over a period longer than other questions because most people don't know what they believe. However, they know what they don't believe. This isn't always good. As a woman, know what you believe and be able to back up that which you believe. However, be open minded to what the individual you are discussing this with believes, and focus on the similarities in your belief instead of the differences.

Question #6: How do you view life after death? This is very important. Many people's actions are based on what and how they view the consequence or the pleasure of their action. A man with a "conscience" will be probably be sincere enough to at least think about the consequences of an adverse action before actually doing it. Not only do you need to know his view of life after death, but how he views the consequences of his actions.

Question #7: Do you pay your tithes and offerings? Many men don't want to give another man money. They may view giving tithes and offerings to a preacher or minister as something that they will not do! I personally believe in the Law of Reciprocity. I also believe in the Bible and Koran's words on giving. Some men believe that if they have to go to work, that their preacher or pastor should also. I advise all of them to read and re-read the throughout the scriptures, especially the book of Malachi chapter 3 and the 31st Chapter of the Koran. There is so much spiritual growth connected with giving, and to the giving of tithes and offerings.

Question #8: **Did you pray with your family on a regular basis growing up?** "A family that prayers together stays together." If a man grew up praying with his family, he will more than likely continue prayer throughout his life. As far back as I can remember, which is as early as about 2 years old, my family (both immediate and extended) prayed. My Great-Grandfather was definitely praying man! I remember being very young, and learning how to pray.

Prayer is better than sleep! It energizes the spirit. If the spirit is energized, the body and the mind can do some powerful things, even if they are both tired.

Question #9: Do you really have the mind of Christ?
This is an important question because an individual that has
the mind of Christ has some real power. The Bible says,
"Let this mind be in you, the same that was in Christ Jesus."
Christ was highly favored by the Creator! In both the Bible
and the Koran, his wonderful works are mentioned. We
are supposed to be able to do even greater than that which
he did. It is very important to know the answer to this
question. Make sure that you have the mind of Christ yourself. Believe the power that was given to Christ, but believe in the power that has been given to you, and then use
it for the benefit of the human family.

Chapter 6

9 Sexual Questions that you must ask

Question #1: **How many women have you had sex with?** This is a very important question to ask. It is a very important question to ask for many reasons. I will tell you a few. I once heard a man say that when he was younger he didn't understand why he was not supposed to have sex before marriage. Now in his mid 30's to early 40's, with a beautiful family, he says he now understands. He expressed that the more people you are sexually involved with before marriage, the harder it is for you to settle down and be committed to one person once you finally decide to do so.

Many of you reading this like to eat sweets. We have all been told that too much sugar is not good for us. If you've had a craving for sugar, you'll agree that when you want it, you want it. You'll get it from anywhere. You just want to fill your craving at that time. Most of the time, after eating it you don't feel good physically or mentally. You begin to tell yourself that you won't do that again. Unfortunately, this is the same way sex before marriage is. You most of the time just want to fill a natural desire for sex that hasn't been fulfilled. You may try and fill this craving with something that looks good, but usually ends up being not so good. Most of the time a man is only looking to fill this craving. Then, when he is done he disposes of the wrapper (you) and waits until he gets another craving or sees a shinier package. The sad part is that more and more women in society are becoming like this, and what's even worse is that it is being widely accepted. No religion that I know of condones being promiscuous.

Question #2: **How old were you when you first had sex?** The interesting part about this is that the people who start having sex at a very young age, may also end up having children at a young age. Before finishing high school; some people before even getting out of junior high, had already lost their virginity. There was so much talk about having sex in school when I was in high school and even in the sixth grade, that I can't believe that more girls I knew didn't get pregnant. The other part to this is that the guys were trying to get the girls that had not had sex to have sex, and the girls were trying to get the guys that had not had sex to have sex. The fact than an individual started having sex at an early age doesn't mean they can't be a good choice for you. However, be careful, because the need to express themselves in this way has been instilled in them, and also may go hand in hand with the above Question #1.

I remember this girl I was courting in the 10th grade that had already been with five guys, and I had been with no one and she wanted to be with me. She was a beautiful young lady with a good heart and everything, but I just wasn't about to get involved further at that point. She also ended up having a few children before I ended up graduating from college. Because of her up bringing I believe she did get married. Mind you, I am not judging her, or anyone for that matter. My oldest sister, youngest sister, and my mother, all had their first child out of wedlock. Much of that had to do with them being naïve and listening to the slick talking of a male. However, from that, I have wonderful nephews that I get to help shape and mold.

Question #3: **What does having sex with someone mean to you?** Some women will read this question and act as if sex doesn't mean anything to them. It's natural in you to want to feel close to a man and vice versa. Make sure that you are thinking and looking out for yourself for the long-term. Make sure that your decision to move forward with this individual is not all based upon emotion and sex. Sex and emotions tend to sometimes blind judgment. With this question, and most of the other questions, don't just take the first answer that the individual gives as "the answer." Please refer back to chapter 2 of the book when I said, "you must become an interview expert." The way great companies get the best of employees is to delve into the thinking of a person. Of course, they usually do this through the process of a series of interviews. Make sure you and the man are in agreement with this question. You may give yourself to him thinking that he views you and the giving of your body to him as special, but in actuality he doesn't.

Question #4: **Have you had or do you desire to have sex with another male?** Also can be asked: Are you on the down low? This question is one that you must really be careful with, and you must bring it up in a way that you actually don't ask the person the question. I would actually advise bringing it up in a couple of conversations. Say something like, "I was reading… or I was listening to…, and they were talking about down low men or bisexual men. What do you think about that?"

His response should give you insight to how he really feels. It's not fair for a woman to have to deal already with what they feel to be the threat of other women, but now the threat of men that portray themselves as straight. This is the reason that question #9 from the Chapter 5 is so important. If a man has the mind of Christ, this wouldn't be an issue. If he has a strong enough desire to overcome this, he can and will overcome it. Chapter 27 verse 55 of the Holy Koran asks a question: "Will you come to men lustfully rather than women?" It then makes a statement..."Nay you are a people who act ignorantly."

Question #5: **Have you ever been sexually abused by anyone?** This is another issue that you may want to be very careful with bringing up. Take the same approach as Question #4. I found out that friends of mine and other people I knew had been sexually abused. I also found out that an individual that was part of a mentor program for young children had picked a few of us out that he had his eye on to try and harm, but thank God that was derailed. This man did end up hurting some other young males years down the line. It also came to my knowledge that he was sent to jail for the acts that he did. This is why it is very important to know the individual that you are involved with. Someone that has been sexually abused may have some issues with sex and being intimate and/or becoming close with someone. Many of you reading this may know first hand, the destructiveness of sexual abuse in its simplistic or most complex form. For both male and female, this can come from a male or female. At any rate, know that this is another issue that you may have to deal with. It doesn't mean that this individual will have a problem relating sexually to you, but this may be something that you may have to work through.

Question #6: **Have you sexually abused anyone?** Ask this question, yet you also have to figure this out by paying attention to the sexually aggressive nature of the individual. Sexual abuse is not the same as sexual aggressiveness. Nonetheless, there is a thin line when it comes to the two, even when individuals are in a relationship or not.

The other issue is not being in a relationship and telling a person "No" to sex. And they tell you, "Yes, you are going to have sex with me after all I did, etc., etc., etc.!!!" This is why you shouldn't go out with a man for extended periods of time, let him spend his money on you, and really begin to fall very much in love with you. If your intentions are to just let him spend money on you and not be working towards a relationship, you may need to rethink this. If you didn't know, I'm letting you know that it is not a wise thing to do. You are putting yourself in a predicament that is not a safe one when you're dealing with the wrong individual. Be careful of who you let in your life especially when it concerns men. (The interesting part about this is that I took a break from writing and begin to watch TV, and America's Most Wanted was about a man who sexually abused people. Two of the young ladies that worked for the guy mentioned how he would be sexually aggressive with them. They also mentioned how smooth and unassuming he was.) Take

Question #7: **How do you feel about being sexually faithful to one woman?** You can think of other ways of saying this. I like this way because it is what is called an "OPEN-ENDED" question. Ask the questions in this book throughout a period of courtship of however long you decide for yourself, and ask them in other ways at different times to see if you get the same or a very similar response. You need to really sit back and listen when he begins talking about this because it will open up to you a wealth of knowledge about this person as an individual. It should also give you insight to what he wants sexually, will give sexually, and tolerate sexually.

The individual you take the opportunity to get to know is the one you choose to get to know. So, don't be upset with him if you find out something you didn't like. Especially, if you didn't ask before you had sex with them. Also, if man tells you that he has not been sexually faithful to one woman, please don't think you can change him. Don't' be fooled if he blames his being unfaithful in relationships on the other women. If a man tells you, "They just weren't the right women for me," please proceed with caution. If he says this you may want to ask him, "What kind of woman is right for you?" Then ask, Well, what kind of women were the women in your past?" If a man is at least man enough to admit to you that in the past I did make some mistakes, of which I have learned from, and I am trying to do better, this may be one that you can continue to get to know. I ask you not to lead him into admitting his mistakes, just because you want him to be something you both know he doesn't desire to be.

Question #8: **How important is having sex in a committed relationship as opposed to having sex and not being in a committed relationship?** Basically you're asking him, "Does it matter whom he gets sex from when he desires to have it?" You want to make sure that the man is the type of man that can and will go to you when he desires intimacy. It is important to be the type of woman that is receptive to her man. You must also ask yourself if you will be the type of woman that just wants intimacy from the person available at that time, or will you go to the man that has committed to you. As long as you don't make a habit of just not being there for him or in the mood, I believe most men can and will understand when you just aren't in the mood for sex. It is not a good idea to make this a habit or try to use not giving him sex (and you are committed to one another) as a means of control.

Ask this question because sex is an actual need whether we want to believe it or not. Years ago, I heard a female minister say, "Sex is as natural as food and water." I was rather young at the time, but this did stick with me. I have read many articles about healthy relationships, and many of them stated a healthy sex life was a very important part of a relationship. In the August 2004 issue of "Redbook Magazine" Jada Pinkett Smith is on the cover, and she has a very interesting story about her and her husband's (Will Smith) relationship. In the article, she talks very much about the ups and downs of their relationship, but she also explains and is open about their sexual relationship. I think it is a great article because sex should be talked about more in the media by people that are actually married.

In our society, the people who talk about sex, having sex, and how good it is and everything, are usually the people who are not even married. I have never been married, but I have been told by a few married friends of mine how much their sex improved once they got married. It actually makes sense because sex was meant to be had with the individual you have made a vow before The Creator and witnesses. It just makes sense. The sad part is many eligible men and women are scared to be married. Many times this is because of some fear put in them by other people or outside forces, whether they want to admit it or not. Therefore, what I have seen is people going from person to person, never being satisfied. As a matter of fact in the same article, Jada speaks about never being one of those women who just had to be married. That's interesting, but I am sure glad she did! She seems to have an outstanding family, and she seems to fit closely to the description of the woman I will go more into detail about in Chapter 14.

Question #9: **What do you think about waiting until getting married before having sex?** This is a good question! I'm actually laughing as I'm writing this. Anyway, if you don't ask any other question in this chapter, ask this one. This will shock him to death! At the same time, ask yourself this question as well. When you ask him this question, just sit back and let him answer. Don't interrupt. Take an agreeable head nodding approach to the response that's given. He'll reveal much with this answer that you need to know as well. Pay attention to what's said, but pay more attention to what is not said and how what is said is said.

Ask this question because you have to know that many men, after they no longer desire to have sex with you will just move on to the next woman. Asking the questions in this book may help keep the man interested in you.

He will probably feel:

      1.She knows what she wants.

          (Which is always an attraction.)

      2.She can hold a decent conversation.

          (Another attraction)

      3.She doesn't only talk about herself, but wants to know about me.

          (10 bonus points)

      4.She's actually kind of smart!

          (This is also a PLUS!!!)

Chapter 7

9 Emotional questions that you must ask

It has been said that there are thousands of words that describe emotions. This means that there are thousands of different emotions that we can experience. Although women are said to be more emotional, believe me when I say men can be just as emotional. When you want to get to know a man you are interested in on an emotional, you may want ask the following questions:

Question #1: **How do you relate to your family?** This is not only referring to his mother and the rest of his immediate family, but his extended family as well. Since it takes a village to raise a child, you need to know how he relates to his grandparents, uncles and aunts, and cousins. If his family is important to him and he takes the time to go see them, or calls regularly, then he more than likely understands the importance of family. Ask him about family reunions or gatherings during the holidays, and pay attention to what his response is. Family is very important when it comes to being emotionally stable and secure about who you are. You may also be able to find out from the family if the person is emotionally stable.

Question #2: **How do you like to express yourself when you feel hurt or upset about something that has been done to you?** Emotional expression is important. When an individual is upset, they may say or do things that they wouldn't normally. You need to know how they express themselves when they are under this type of stress and/or anger. Can also be asked, **"What do you do when you get upset?"**

Question #3: **What is your idea of affection?** How do you like to show affection? Either question will do. If you ask both of these questions just like they are listed, you may learn whether or not he will be able to show you the affection you desire. A man that shows affection to his mother may be the kind of husband that will show affection to his wife.

Question #4: **Do you have a fear of being married?** I probably should have made this the first question of the chapter. His answer to this question should let you know for sure if he will be able to pop the question, if you are looking to be in a long-term relationship with him. Fear is a very strong emotion. However, an even stronger emotion than fear is LOVE. The bible says, perfect love casts out FEAR. If he does have some fear about this, it is usually normal in men. My next book will deal with the reasons why many men don't pop the question of marriage. As you already know, one of those reasons is fear. Many times, there are multiple fears that men have about this. Either way you need to know his response to this question.

F.E.A.R. is False Evidence Appearing Real

Question #5: **How do you like to be consoled and comforted?** Believe it or not, there are many men that enjoy being consoled and comforted. As a matter of fact, I believe Tupac said in one of his songs, "Nothing makes a man feel better than a woman." I would also have to say, "Nothing can make a man feel worse than a woman."

In the book of Proverbs, both of these statements hold true. In Proverbs 21:9, it states, "Better to dwell in a corner of a housetop, Than in a house shared with a contentious woman." In verse 19 of the 21st chapter it says, "Better to dwell in the wilderness, Than with a contentious and angry woman." In another part of Proverbs it goes on to agree with Tupac. Proverbs 31:10-12 states the following: "Who can find a virtuous wife? For her worth is far above rubies. The heart of her husband safely trusts her; So he will have no lack of gain. She does him good and not evil all the days of her life." In the beginning of the bible when God saw that Adam was alone, he gave him Eve. The Holy Koran speaks about God giving man and woman to each other to help give one another "quiet of mind." A man naturally wants to be consoled. It's good for you to find out how the individual would like to be consoled..

Question #6: **What is your idea of happiness? What makes you happy?** The idea of happiness is different when it comes to each individual. For some, being single and being free to sleep with any and every woman that they choose at any time is happiness. For others, it could be to find one woman, no matter her looks, education, or whatever she may have, to just be nice to him. A man could also want to sit at home and do nothing all day and be taken care of by a woman. Whatever it is, you need to find out if you and the man are on the same wave length with your pursuit of happiness.

Don't Worry. Be Happy!

Question #7: **When was the last time you had an argument? Did it lead to physical confrontation?**
You need to know whether or not this or other arguments have led to physical confrontation. If a person has acted out in the past they may have the tendency to go that route again. You also need to find out what happened to cause the last argument. Be careful because if they blame it all on the other individual, this may be a practice they do often no matter what role they played in the argument. If he only speaks of what the other individual did to cause the disagreement, ask the following question: "Do you accept any responsibility for the difficulty?" Listen intently to his answer. It should allow you to understand his ability to accept responsibility for his role in the disagreement. Doing this may show you how humble he is.

Question #8: **What do you love the most?** Remember, Perfect LOVE casts out FEAR! When you love something, you give your time to it, and you take care of it. The Bible states that GOD is LOVE. As I stated earlier, in mathematics the "equal sign" (=) and "is" are the same thing. Don't for one second ignore what he says at this time. A man that may be most in love with himself, may be a little selfish. At the same time, a man that doesn't love himself at all may do destructive actions and think destructive thoughts. Listen for words that have to do with family, goals, long-term desires for his life, and some mention of a higher eternal power when he gives this type of answer.

As with all answers, there is no wrong or right answer. It just depends on what it is that you want. There are certain answers that a man can give that are from the heart, and others that are from his head just to say what you want to hear. For this reason...LISTEN!

Question #9: **What do you fear most?** This is just as important as the above question. The bible says, "The fear of the Lord is the beginning of knowledge." (Proverbs 1:7). A spiritually grounded man should FEAR the Creator of the Heavens and the Earth the most. The Creator should also be what a man loves the most! However, in asking this question, you begin to learn what type of man you are dealing with. What we fear has a means of controlling us and our actions. Many of the men that answer this question may tell you that they aren't afraid of anything. Every man has some fear. Even if the fear that he has is the Lord, he has one and you need to know what he fears. Please understand that certain fears are healthy. However, most of them are not. Knowing what he fears will get you in touch with the side of him that he may not otherwise reveal.

Love is stronger than Fear!

-Armani Valentino-

Chapter 8

9 Physical Questions that you must ask

This chapter deals with the physical make up and attraction of a woman that a man may like. It should also help you to look further than what only your eyes can see. This chapter is important to deal with because many men may never tell you that you are not what he is physically attracted to. He may not be at a level where he knows that a woman is more than physical appearance. It will also help you to learn more about any physical issues he may have that you don't desire to deal with.

"It is only with the heart that one can see rightly;

what is essential is invisible to the eye."

-Antoine De Saint-Exupery-

Question #1: **What type of woman are you usually attracted to?** This should be one of the questions that he will be more than happy to answer. Let him know that you only mean physical attraction if he asks. Most men are physically attracted to many different women. Everyone usually has there ideal person they're physically attracted to. I heard this is usually based on a fantasy idea from childhood. Now, if a man says, "What do you mean?" Or if he says, "Do you mean physically, mentally, spiritually, etc." This may mean that you have run into a man that has some serious game, or he is just a man that appreciates women on all levels.

Question #2: **Do you find yourself physically attractive?** Some of the questions that I am writing, I can't even believe they come to my mind. *LOL*

I actually get to laughing sometimes while writing this book because I would love to see the face of men that get asked certain questions like this one. Anyway, this question comes to mind because I know that some of you are dating or desire to date some guy that just thinks he is God's gift to women. If you are or don't know if you are, you will find out once you ask this question. I was told that there is a fine line between arrogance and confidence. Many of us don't know when we've crossed it.

Question #3: **Do you find me physically attractive? If yes, what makes me physically attractive?** I do warn that when you ask this question, you may not like the answer you get. I also warn you that just because he answers favorably doesn't mean that he is attracted to you. However, if he says "no," it doesn't mean that he is not interested in you. A man can find you attractive, but doesn't have to be attracted you.

Question #4: **What do you think your best physical attributes are?** Whatever answer is given at this time will usually let you know what the individual is most physically confident with. Depending on the answer, the individual may be a little over confident about something that years from now may not be useful. Answers that deal with or entice your sexual imagination, may not be good signs.

Question #5: **What did you get teased about growing up?** This question makes for some interesting conversation. When I was growing up, my skin was something that people teased me about. I had Eczema, and it would get really bad sometimes. The guys used to really tease me., while the young ladies understood and really cared about the condition of my skin improving.

I remember one time I didn't even go to school because it was so bad. After school, a group of female friends came by to see why I wasn't at school, and I hid in the bathroom. The different physical attributes that we get teased about tend to set up self-esteem issues for many of us. Subconsciously the individual may already have issues about this, and you should never tease him about it. I don't care how upset in the future you may get with him, do not tease him.

Never tease a man about a physical condition.

Question #6: **Do you have any physical issues that you have to deal with that most people don't know about?** This is a question that many may not want to answer. You shouldn't ask this question too early in the process. Many people may have some sort of physical condition that may affect their life. This doesn't make someone a bad choice as a mate; it's just something you may need to know if you plan to take the relationship further. As with all of the questions in the book, they are being asked to help you get a better idea of what you may be getting yourself into. The questions aren't for you to judge an individual. Better yet, they are for you to get to know this person before you make the decision to become sexually involved with him. Remember that you are not perfect, and you have your own set of issues that this man may have to deal with as well.

Question #7: **Physically, what do you desire from your partner on a regular basis?** This question will probably get many different responses. He may answer this question and a few of the other questions with a question. Please be careful not to go ahead and answer the question if you get asked a question and yours hasn't been answered. All you need to do is give him an example of what you mean, or just repeat the question in a different way. Different men desire different things. Some may want you to scratch their head or massage their hands when they get off work. Some may want you to hug or kiss them every time they see you. Whatever the person's desires may be, just listen to what they say. It doesn't mean that you have to do these things. However, it may become an issue if you don't want to do these things in a relationship with him.

Question #8: **What do you physically like to do for your partner on a regular basis?** When you see questions like this one and #7, they are in that order for a reason. If you want to know certain things, you must understand the "Art of asking Questions" as discussed earlier in Chapter 2. You are setting him up to find out something that you need to know. Overall, most women want to treat a man well. However, many women haven't received good treatment in return from a man. When you ask a man what he wants, then turn around and ask him what he likes to give, you set a rule in his mind early on in the relationship. The rule that you set up is, "There is no such thing as something for nothing." We live in a universe that has certain laws. Many of these laws are discussed in the scriptures.

This particular law that you are teaching him is called the **"Law of Reciprocity."** Many men have the thought that there are no consequences or responsibility of sleeping with a woman. Please know what I mean when I say this. They think it's all just free. I was told, "Romance without finance, is a nuisance." It couldn't be truer. As a man, I am just trying to give you more insight as to why what a man is willing to do for you, is just as important as what you are willing to do for him. A relationship is a two-way street.

Question #9: **How often do you bathe?** This is one of the questions that you can ask on any date you choose, including the first one. This is also another one of those questions that I can't believe I am telling you to ask. This is a very important one to ask. I am going to be very open with you right now. Many of you reading this may be in college, and may not know that the guy you are dating may not take a bath every day. This same guy may not see anything wrong with this.

Hygiene is a very important part of being around someone. Sometimes, you may find a guy that is nice, has money, and is single. Don't always be so happy to find this because his hygiene may be the reason why he doesn't have someone. Instead of telling him, everyone has just let him continue to go on smelling how he smells. If you really like a guy and his hygiene is the issue, just let him know. Say something like, "Hey, I really like you. I would like to continue getting to know you. And I would like you so much more if you were to take better care of your hygiene."

There is no guarantee what the response will be, but he may actually listen if he really likes you. He may actually thank you. If his hygiene is the issue, the best way he can thank you is to do something about it. If he still doesn't get it, ask yourself if you can get used to his hygiene.

Chapter 9

9 Health Questions that you must ask

Just because a person appears physically fit, doesn't mean that they are healthy. Fitness is "the physical ability to perform athletic activity." Health, is defined as "the state where all the systems of the body – nervous, muscular, skeletal, circulatory, digestive, lymphatic, hormonal, etc. – are working in an optimal way." * Please note that when asking these questions, you want to make sure you understand that most people at some point in their lives will have some sort of issue with their health. You shouldn't rule out the individual you are interested in just because he has a health issue and you don't. On the other hand, know what you are willing to deal with and what you aren't willing to deal with. Just be open, and understanding.

Question #1: **How important is exercise to you?** Exercise is a huge part of being healthy. It is not health itself, but it is a great part of maintaining an overall healthy lifestyle. Exercise releases endorphins to the brain, which have been said to be more powerful than morphine. Exercise is supposed to make you feel good. It builds confidence, endurance, gives you energy. In its aerobic form, it helps to improve the heart, lungs, blood vessels, and muscles. An individual that exercises or does some sort of aerobic activity on a regular basis may be able to stay committed to and develop other healthy habits. On the other hand, someone that exercises absolutely too much, may not understand the principle of doing things in moderation.

*From the book, "Awaken the Giant Within, by Anthony Robbins. © Copyright.1991.Anthony Robbins.

*Maffetone, Dr. Philip, Everyone Is an Attitude, New York: David Barmore Publishers, 1990

Question #2 – When was the last time you had a physical checkup? Men probably don't get check ups near as much as women. I don't know the actual figures on this, but I can almost be sure that we don't. Physical check ups are important. They help us keep track of where we are in our physical realm of health. The person that has a routine check up is more than likely concerned about being and living healthy. It is much easier to be happier if you are healthy.

-from 3 John 1:2-
Beloved, I wish above all things
that thou mayest prosper and be in health...

Question #3 – When was the last time you had a basic STD test? This is a question that must be asked. Many people think that as long as a person is HIV negative, that they are okay to sleep with. There are far more STDs than AIDS or HIV. I would hope that the Black women reading this book would also note that HIV/AIDS as a whole is down, but in black women it is up(at the time of this writing). Therefore, please try your best to get a good answer to this question. If the both of you have to go to get tested together, I believe that this is a good thing. Just understand the importance of it, and don't overlook this question. If it has been more than a year and the individual has had multiple partners, you should encourage them to get tested. It would be a good thing for their overall health and well being. Also, ask him to share the results. Ask this question once you are genuinely interested in moving into a relationship with the individual.

Question #4: **Do you smoke? Do you do drugs? This can be cigarettes, marijuana, cocaine, etc.** Can also be asked...*How do you feel about smoking cigarettes, marijuana, etc.?* Whether you smoke or not, ask the individual this question. This question can save you some disappointment. Many times the individual can hide this for a long time. If you are a smoker you need to ask this question because the individual may not desire to be with some that smokes. The long term effects of smoking are terrible. I watched a very beautiful woman die at a somewhat early age from smoking. It was horrible. Her daughter was devastated. If the man likes to smoke or use other drugs, you need to know this. If you don't do these things, it is best to get with someone that doesn't. On the other hand if you do, make sure that this individual you are talking to doesn't see it as an issue if he doesn't do it. Don't judge him if you don't. Don't choose to be with a man that smokes if you know you don't desire it. The bottom line is, smoking negatively effects your health.

Question #5: **How do you feel about getting drunk on a regular basis?** Do you drink? Have you ever been drunk? You may drink or you may not. Either way, just like smoking, drinking alcohol or other intoxicants can have negative side effects. I heard Zig Ziglar say, "One in nine social drinkers become alcoholics." That was in the 90's when I heard that particular recording that he did. The numbers are probably fairly close to that still, if not worse. Drinking too much is not a responsible act.

I worked as a national sales recruiter for a great company. Many of the companies wouldn't hire you if you had a DUI or DWI. Not only does getting drunk possibly hurt your health, but it also can hurt you financially. In the book of Proverbs, chapter 31, King Lemuel shares some of the utterances of his mother. In verses 4 & 5 the following is stated: 4) "It is not for kings, O Lemuel, It is not for kings to drink wine, Nor for Princes intoxicating drink; 5) Lest they drink and forget the law, And pervert the justice of all the afflicted." Obviously his mother, as the queen at the time when she told him these things, knew what would help him as a prince and a king. For those of you who read the Koran, in Chapter 5 (The Food) verse 91 it reads: "The devil desires only to create enmity and hatred among you by means of intoxicants and games of chance, and to keep you back from the remembrance of Allah (God) and from prayer. Will you then keep back?" Both Bible and Koran agree when it comes to this.

Question #6: **Is there any history of diabetes, epilepsy, asthma, or any other illness that could be detrimental to you?** Ask this question only after knowing the person for more than a month. You ask this question not to be nosey, but for your own knowledge just in case something happens while you are out with him. By knowing this he may be able to let you know in advance what to do just in case. At this time, if you have any problems such as these or any others, you also need to let the individual know. This is not usually a huge issue, but can become one if you don't know.

Question #7: **What are you favorite foods to eat? What is your favorite meal?** Knowing what a person's favorite food items to eat also help you get a glimpse into their habits. Good food and eating habits usually transfer into other areas of life. An individual can have other good habits if they like to eat sweets all the time, or red meat, or junk food. I read an article in Ebony Magazine about super-producer, Rodney Jerkins (also known as Darkchild). In the article, he expressed how he lost 100 pounds. He expressed even more so why he lost the weight and what it did for his focus, mental strength, life, and musical creativity. He also expressed how his music has gone to a whole new level because of his eating habits. The daily diet that he previously had was not conducive to his overall health. Once he changed his eating habits, instead of just going on a diet to lose weight, he was able to not only lose the 100 pounds, but he has kept it off. From this, I believe that he would agree when I say, "you are what you eat." Congratulations to you Mr. Jerkins. You look like a brand new man! And from the article I read, you sound like a new man.

Question #8: **What foods are off limits for you?** Everyone should have something that they just will not eat. We are not animals. We should not eat everything. As a matter of fact, most animals have something that they just will not eat. This question is a good question because if the both of you decide to go out to eat or you cook for him, you need to know this. Some people have certain health conditions that won't allow them to eat certain things. Others may have religious beliefs that are against certain foods.

More and more people are becoming vegetarians. More men are not eating red meat now-a-days. I believe that LL Cool J has openly expressed that he was a vegetarian. The man looks like he is about 21 years old, and he is over 35. He always seems fairly happy, has a wonderful attitude, and the ladies love him! Having limits when it comes to food is a good thing.

You are what you eat.

Question #9: **Can you cook? If so, how often do you cook? How often do you eat out?** I know this is more than one question, but all of them need to be asked, or two of them if the man can't cook. A man that can take the time to cook food for himself, will more than likely take time to do the same for you from time to time. A man that can cook usually enjoys home cooked meals more so than eating out. He may also know the effect that eating out has on the health of a financial budget.

Most of the time when people eat out, they aren't eating at some extravagant restaurant that serves full course meals. They are usually eating, pizza, burgers, sandwiches, fries, hot wings, hot dogs, chips, and a soft drink. These food items don't take long to prepare, and the damage that they do to the body on a regular basis is not good. If you haven't watched the documentary, "Super Size Me" you need to. The Bible speaks of your body as being a temple, so why not try it that way. You should also help the man of your interest do the same if he doesn't already.

Chapter 10

9 Financial Questions that you must ask

Finances are mentioned in the Bible and Koran numerous times. In relationships, the main problems that people tend to have are said to be money related. I recently saw a book from two authors and very successful businessmen. I didn't get to read the book, but I believe that the title of the book was, "Why We Want You to be Rich," by Donald Trump and Robert Kiyosoki. I could only imagine what the book was about. Money is an important factor in the success or failure of certain relationships. However, to keep relationships together, it takes much more than money.

A feast is made for laughter, and wine makes merry;

But MONEY answers everything.

-Ecclesiastics 10:19-

"The man is the maintainer of the woman..."

-from the Holy Koran Chapter 4:34-

Question #1: **How old were you when you first started working?** The earlier a person is when they begin to develop a good work ethic, the easier it should become for them to want to work. In Donald Trump's book, "How to Get Rich," he also agrees that an individual should start working at a very young age. People in times before ours got married at much earlier ages than many of us do now. Because the individuals were reared to begin working at an early age, they learned how to take care of and financially provide for a family. There is still truth in this today.

Question #2: Do you pay tithes and offerings? Do you give to charity? This goes back to the Law of Reciprocity that I spoke of earlier. In the Koran, Chapter 6 verse 161 it reads; Whoever brings a good deed will have tenfold like it, and whoever, brings an evil deed, will be recompensed only with the like of it, and they shall not be wronged." The Bible says, "He who has a generous eye will be blessed, for he gives of his bread to the poor." A man that knows the principles of giving and practices them, will obviously be a blessed man that will be blessed with much more than what he gives. In this book, many scriptures are sometimes used to back up certain points, so that if you say you believe in the scriptures, you will understand that much of what I have been given to write to you are timeless pieces of wisdom from the Creator's chosen vessels. Pay your tithes. Go read the third chapter of Malachi. Pay attention to the question that it asks, "Will a man rob God?"

Question #3: Do you have a checking account? Savings? Other investments? The interesting part about this is that many people don't have a checking account. Having one is important. If you want to have and keep some money, most bankers and wealthy individuals would say begin with a bank account, both checking and savings. Learn to manage your money by paying yourself at least 10% of every dollar you make, and don't touch it. After a while, you will begin to see your money grow. A man that spends everything today to keep up with the rest of the crowd may not have anything tomorrow. If he doesn't have a bank account, find out why and see if he can be helped.

Question #4: **Do you have health & life insurance?** This is important. We can leave this earth at anytime. We can get sick at anytime. Having insurance, even if it is only a small amount is important. If you are at the point of marriage planning with this individual, you may need to get more. The idea of "I am not going to leave this earth anytime soon" may often go through a vibrant and healthy man's mind. If he has considered this and is taking steps toward obtaining insurance, he is probably a man that thinks ahead. If he already has some insurance...GREAT!

Question #5: **How well do you enjoy your current occupation?** If the person is a full-time student ask them, '**What are your plans after high school and/or college?** " A person that enjoys what they do usually finds a way to make a good living at it. If not, you may see a very unhappy individual working to pay bills, and not because they enjoy it. They may go to work to do just enough to keep from getting fired. This type of person may also stay in a relationship just because they have gotten used to it, and may only do just enough to keep the other person around.

Question #6: **Do you own or rent?** If you rent, **Do you have any plans to own a home, condo, or a townhouse in the future?** If so, **When do you plan to do so?** Many people rent. However, if you plan on getting anywhere financially, as taught by my finance professor, Dr. Jules King, you must own some real estate. Even if the real estate that you own is being rented to someone else, you need to find a way to own some real estate.

Everyone that has a place to stay participates in real estate. They participate in real estate willingly or unwillingly. Why not want to own some real estate and get with a man that desires to own some real estate as well. Together, you can do it.

Question #7: **How's your credit?** I don't know the statistics, but I am almost sure more women have better credit than men. If this is true for you, you may have to help him get his credit together. Is there anything wrong with this? Well, I think that would depend on you. You must first make sure that he is the type of man that is willing to listen, and be appreciative of your help. You don't have to fix it for him, but lead him in the right direction. You may be the woman that has bad credit, and need his help. Either way, this shouldn't be a disqualifier for a committed relationship. This is just something that you need to know in advance. As long as a workable plan can be put together and followed, there is hope for credit problems. One time, I heard a girl say to her friend while I was out selling CDs, "Girl he's driving a XYZ car, his credit ain't good enough to be talking to me. He can't even co-sign." I thought this was so funny, but in a sense it made sense. You need to know what his credit is like, but at the same time, know that this is something that can be fixed. *Some things can't be fixed.* So if you find a man that has all these other good qualities you are looking for, but find out he has not so good credit, don't count him out.

CREDIT can be IMPROVED!

Question #8: **How do you feel about women making more money than men?** This is a tricky question. In our society today, we have many women making just as much if not more than men. This is an issue in some cases. This may also cause friction in some cases because a man may be easily controlled by a woman that may make more money than him. I am not saying that this is always the case, but it can create some issues in a marriage and other relationships. In Corinthians it says, "that the Head of every man is Christ, the head of woman is man, and the head of Christ is God." I once heard a great minister say, "He can't be the head if he doesn't have a head." Funny, but true. I've known many women that have married a man that didn't have much money, but he had the potential to have much and just needed a little help. Those men now take very good care of their wife.

If I remember properly, I heard Denzel Washington speak about his wife in an interview. He expressed how he thought he had to have "Everything Together" before he could get married. He felt that he didn't have it together and wanted to wait. I believe that he then expressed how she explained to him that this is not how things work. I have heard it said, "Beside every strong man is an even stronger woman."

In the Bible, the part about Eve coming from the rib of Adam is a symbol of the importance and also the place where the woman should be with her man. She shouldn't be behind him or in front of him, but right beside him. Then, when she is not right beside her man, she begins to listen to the slinking snake devil whisper in her ear.

She gets spiritually bit, and poisons her man with the same venom that she received from Satan. If you know the man you desire has real potential, it may be good to stick with him and not listen to the whispers of those with evil intentions. Help him, but make sure that if you make more money than him, you don't use your money as a means of control.

Ecclesiastics 4:9-11 reads; 9) "Two are better than one, because they have a good reward for their labor. 10) For if they fall, one will lift up his companion. But woe to him ho is alone when he falls, for he has no one to help him up. 11) Again, for if two lie down together, they will keep warm; But how can one be warm alone?" Those of you who are women that do make more than the man you desire to be with, understand that even with all your money and luxuries, "Two are better than one."

Question #9: **Where do you see yourself in the next 5 years or 10 years?** You don't need to ask this question until you have asked the rest of them in this chapter. The answer to this question will pretty much let you see whether or not he meant most of what he was saying. **"Where there is no vision the people perish."** The answer should coincide with most of the answers given to the rest of the questions. If they don't, he may not be telling you the truth. This may also allow you to know if some of the other answers that he gave to other questions in other chapters were truthfully answered. Listen! You must realize how important it is for you to listen, remember, and pay attention to the answers.

If you pay attention, you may find out **"You're just not that into him."** To the men reading this book, "It's time to step your game way up!"

Personal Statement & Commitment to LOVE

Write your name in the blank below:

I _____ choose to be Love's expression. I commit daily to share, give, and receive love. By doing this, I am going to improve who I am. By properly loving myself, I will be able to better love The Creator of the Heavens and Earth, my family, my friends, my community, my nation, my fellowman, and the World. This love will cause me to make better decisions about my overall health, mental, emotional, spiritual, financial, sexual, educational, family, relationship, and physical well-being. And like the Sun, my love will shine bright and radiate to rest of the world. I understand that love is the most powerful energy in the Universe. Therefore, I choose to be Love's expression.

Write this on an index card or read it from the book, and keep it in your pocket, wallet, bag, or purse. Read it out loud with feeling when you first wake up, around lunch time, and before you go to bed every night. Do this for 9 days, and you should notice a positive change in your attitude about life. Do it for 18 days, and others around you should notice the improvement. Do it for 27 days, and it should become automatic; you should also notice a huge improvement in your attitude about "LOVE" and "LIFE."

When you commit to this and follow through, 9 days after you begin I want to hear from you. In 18 days, I want to hear from you. In 27 days, I want to hear from you.
Email me at: info@armanivalentino.com

Show & Tell

Instructions: Below are two columns that you will write 9 names on each side. The first column will be the names of 9 ladies you believe could benefit from this book in some way. The other side will be the names of 9 women or men you don't believe could benefit from reading this book.

1.) _____   1.) _____

2.) _____   2.) _____

3.) _____   3.) _____

4.) _____   4.) _____

5.) _____   5.) _____

6.) _____   6.) _____

7.) _____   7.) _____

8.) _____   8.) _____

9.) _____   9.) _____

Now that you have finished, contact each individual listed in both columns and let them see the book. Don't let them borrow it, you may not get it back. *LOL*

Every individual you listed will more than likely be able to benefit from the book, including those that seem to be in a happy marriage or relationship.

Chapter 11

9 Education Questions that you must ask

Education is a lifelong process. Once you stop learning you begin to digress. Knowledge is everywhere, and knowledge is the foundation of education. It is infinite, and it always has been. Therefore, to stop learning in a time like today is actually a detriment to the individual that does.

In his book, "Torchlight for America," Minister Louis Farrakhan, who has been widely misunderstood, discusses the problems with the educational system in our country. Unlike some people, he also offers some real workable solutions. I hope that this book you are reading right now helps to solve some problems in another educational way for men and women alike.

Education is a lifelong process.

Question #1: **How often do you read? Do you like to read?** In the book, Torchlight for America, I remember much about the "functionally illiterate." Years ago, I didn't know what functionally illiterate meant. I thought that if you could read that was all you needed. In the book it mentioned how a large part of the population could read, but not grasp most of what they read. Most of the time when people aren't that good at something, they don't usually like to do it that often. If you read more, you will become better at it. Reading is something that I hope our society gets more and more back into. Growing up knowing how to read at a very young age made me feel that anything was possible. The books that I read helped to develop my imagination. In his book, "What Makes the Great Great?," Dr. Dennis Kimbro, speaks on the power of the imagination.

Reading helps to tremendously improve the imagination. If a man loves to read, he may want to spend time with his children reading to them and helping them with their homework when that time comes. Motivational Extraordinaire, "Tony Robbins," believes that "Readers are Leaders." Damon Dash, co-founder of Roc-A-Fella Records & Roc-A-Wear Brand, on his Reality TV show, the "Ultimate Hustler," expressed the importance of reading the latest magazines and news about his industry, in order to stay educated on the latest information and trends.

Question #2: **What was your favorite subject growing up? Why?** A person may answer this question in many ways. The answer to this question should let you know what area (s) the person is most confident in as far as their knowledge is concerned.

Question #3: **What is the name of your favorite book?** If he says the Bible or Koran, this is great, but don't be fooled by the answer. Ask him, "Which book of the bible or chapter of the Koran?" As with the food you eat physically, you are what you eat. We are also what eat on a spiritual and educational plateau as well. Not only is it important to know if a man reads, but if so, "What is he reading?"

Question #4: **Do you have plans to continue your education?** Whatever the level of education that an individual is at right now you need to know if they plan to continue beyond their current status.

As stated earlier, education is a lifelong process. Even if a person just wants to continue learning how to type better, get certified to cut hair, fix cars, or anything that will keep them learning, it's good. Even teachers, have to continue their education for years after they've graduated college. They have many workshops to keep them up-to-date on the latest knowledge for their students.

Question #5: **Where did you go to college and Why? Did you graduate?** This is if the person went. If the person didn't go, ask them, **"Why did you choose not to attend?** Whether or not the person chose to go to college, it's not a bad thing. Some of the greatest men and women in our society didn't go. Other Greats didn't finish. Ask these questions to get an idea of where the person's thinking was once they finished high school (if they finished). This should be a good way to help you evaluate their thought process. Some people decided to do other things like the military, and many of the other things stated earlier instead of going to a Community College or 4-year University. Many of these people that didn't go may now be making a decent amount of money.

Question #6: **Do you like to travel? Where have you had the opportunity to travel to?** A person that has had the opportunity to travel outside their region, may have a bigger picture of what the world is like. Their possibilities are usually broadened, and their goals and dreams seem to be more achievable. It also helps them to become more cultured. Traveling helps to expand your imagination.

When I've had the opportunity to travel, it has opened my eyes and mind to the similarities and minor differences of the different races, cultures, and backgrounds of the world. That in itself is EDUCATION.

Question #7: **What magazines do you subscribe to or like to read?** I have found a wealth of information in many, many, magazines and newspapers. Most magazines offer information that definitely helps to expand the mind. Others may be strictly for entertainment purposes only. Magazines are read widely by individuals from all walks of life. Many of the people that write for magazines are experts in a particular field. Once again, knowing what a person likes to read may help to understand them and their basis of knowledge.

Question #8: **How often do you watch TV? What are your favorite shows to watch?** It has been said that we watch an enormous amount of television in America. Most of what is watched is not conducive to improving an individual's life. Television is a powerful influence on the mind. I now know why the magician's and stunt men on TV say "Don't try this at home." Many of the young children will try and imitate what is seen on TV, and some adults may try to do the same. Television influences the fashion, music, language, and the overall lifestyle of the majority of the population. Therefore, it is a tool that actually teaches certain behaviors. It is an educational tool. Learn what he watches, and you may see many of his actions influenced by the programs he watches.

Question #9: What kind of music do you listen to? What is your favorite station? Who are your favorite music artist? Just as television influences, so does music. I am an artist that has performed across the US with my singing group BWP. We have seriously been able to influence many people's lives. Many of the schools that we performed in, the young people, remembered us years down the road. One time, we were in the audience at a high school talent show. We were there only to support a few of the younger artists performing. One of the artists was Mike D.'s little brother, and another artist was a group of young men that actually won the talent show. This particular group of young men had won the talent show two years prior to this by singing one of our songs. This particular year they had decided to sing our latest song, "One of These Days," a ballad about being with someone, wanting to be married and staying together. They won their category and the overall contest once again with our song. That's influence. Someone found out that we were in the audience, and asked us to come and sing. We did one of our songs from 3 or 4 years prior to that and the crowd of about 400 people loved it and most of them actually knew the words and sang along. This was phenomenal to me because we weren't some famous group. However, the influence from when we used to sing to them when they were in junior high was still there. Music is powerful, and it is important to know what he listens to. More than likely, if he listens to music that is constantly calling women, "B@#ch$ & gardening tools," this may be what he will think of you.

Chapter 12

9 Family Questions that you must ask

The Family is the backbone of any nation. Once the family unit begins to breakdown, that nation will follow suit. Strong families make strong communities. Strong communities make strong cities. Strong cities make strong states. Strong states definitely make strong nations. The family unit is very important. Many of the problems that we face in our country are due to the lack of families being there for one another, families not staying together and standing strong in times of difficulty, as well as times of joy.

Question #1:   **How important is your family?** The answer to this question, should guide you into the knowledge of whether or not this man is marriage material.

Earlier today, I was watching OPRAH, and I had the opportunity to see an interview with Chris Rock. It was a great interview! I absolutely loved it! In the interview you could see the importance of his family. It was genuine, and he didn't even have to say that he loved his wife or children. You could see that he loved them and they loved him. There was a part about going to the school that Oprah opened up in South Africa. In this particular section, he picked up the book he brought to donate to the library, and it was a children's book. He expressed how he had wanted to have children so bad that he had bought that particular book before he and his wife had their girls. He also expressed how his father used to look at them whenever he would get off work and just stare at them.

He didn't know what it meant then, but now that he was a father, he seemed to have a better understanding of his father's position as a father. He spoke of how he could just talk for hours and hours about his family. It was real and genuine! I loved the interview and it made me definitely know that as a young man, desiring a family is a good thing.

Question #2: What was it like growing up in your household? For some people, things were great and for others it was terrible. Either way, this is something that you need to know as a woman if you desire to be in a committed marriage or committed long-term relationship. An individual will either mimic what went on in their household or try and do the exact opposite. I know an older gentleman whose father wasn't there tell me, "The fact of my father not being around made me want to be everything opposite of what he was." This was good! He has a beautiful wife and two boys that are out of high school, and doing well. One of them started on the football team as a freshman at Boston College. The other I believe is becoming an electrician. Either way, he took the experience that he had growing up and turned it for the better. The positive or negative effect of their upbringing is very important.

Question #3: How many brothers and sisters do you have? Men that grow up with other females in the house may have the tendency to think twice about how they treat other women. They would know that women have feelings, and they are not toys to be played with.

Am I saying that if a man didn't have any sisters he can't respect women? No. Conversely, the thought may come to a man's mind, "What if someone was to do my sister like this?" This leads me to my next question...

Question #4: **How well do you get along with the female members of your family? How do you feel about the females in your family?** If he doesn't have any sisters, you can still ask this question because he may have female cousins and aunts. When asking this question, listen to how he expresses his love and appreciation for them. I asked a friend this question, and with the first question he just gave a simple answer. So I asked the next question. He told me how much he cared about them, loved them, would protect them, and do anything for them. His answer was genuine. It wasn't scripted because my call actually woke him up. He wasn't expecting it. Therefore, ask both questions if you get a very simple non-expressive answer on the first question.

Question #5: If he has children, **"Do you have any girls?"** If he doesn't have any children and wants some, ask him, **"Would you like to have any girls?"** There is a radio DJ in my hometown named Sean Michaels. He probably won't remember telling me this, but years ago, we were talking about women and how they were being disrespected in music. At this time, he was telling me how he didn't really look at women the same as he used to because he now had a daughter of his own.

Question #6: **What do you know about your grandparents and ancestors?** I heard a speech that Malcolm X did about history. In the speech, he spoke about the importance of knowing your ancestry. He said that what made royalty; royalty was that they knew their ancestry. It made sense. Many people have no earthly idea who their great grandparents were. If they do, they know very little about their life. Recently, Rev. Al Sharpton, a known activist for Civil Rights, found out that his ancestry linked him and a long-time senator that at one time was totally for segregation. He expressed how shocking it was. It did however; let him know more about himself.

The interesting part about knowing much of your family history is that it gives you a sense of purpose. It helped me to know that my life is definitely not mine alone, and that many generations paid a serious price for me to be here today. I know that there are many men and women that paid with their prayers, life, sacrifices, and everything to hope that life would one day be better for me. A man that has this kind of pride about himself, may likely desire to continue to set up a stronger foundation for his future generations with a woman that desires the same.

Know thyself.
-Socrates-

Question # 7: **Do you see yourself starting your own family? How do you feel about one day starting your own family?** The answer to this question in particular, should coincide with the first question in the next chapter. So please pay attention to the answer that the man gives you at this point. If you don't desire what he desires in this area, you may not need to move forward with him being a possible partner for you. A man that is usually serious about desiring a family, may also be serious about playing his role very well in that family.

Question #8: **Does your family have family reunions? If so, "Do you attend?" or "Well, tell me about the reunions. What kinds of things do you all do?"** Another friend of mine was quizzed by me on this particular question, and didn't even know it was one of the questions in the book. I asked him the questions in the order that they are typed above, and he gave me what I needed to know. I was able to understand just how much he loved his family. Many other men may respond to you in the same manner. If the man has been to family reunions, you may want to ask him other questions about some of his favorite times, and favorite family members. This is just to help you get a general idea about his take on family, and how sincere most of the other answers to questions in this chapter are.

You just have to make sure that you bring it up in regular conversation. Please try your best not to sound rehearsed. The questions have been sectioned off by subject matter to help you not sound so scripted.

For example: If you and I are talking about the All-Star game, certain things come up while talking about the game. If we both watched it, things may come up like, did you see the dunk XYZ player did, or I can't believe the East or West lost.

Question #9: **Are your mother and father still together?** If not, it would be wise to find out why they're not. It may make a difference in him wanting to stay in a committed or believing that people can actually stay together and be happy. If one parent or both parents have passed away, this may be a touchy subject for him, so please be careful. I know first hand about the psychological effects of parents splitting up. Some friends of mine watched their parents split at a time in their life when they needed both parents. The two I can think of are still affected by it right now. Because they had this picture of what they thought was a perfect family, and then all of the sudden that picture was shattered, they now have to deal with the broken glass. Although they are adults now, it still hurts and has had a huge impact on how they relate to the opposite sex.

Note: Try to ask questions by chapters, and usually in the order in which they are listed in each chapter.

Chapter 13

9 Relationship Questions that you must ask

The root word of relationship is relation. In the American Heritage Dictionary, Third Edition, one of the definitions for the word relation is: "A logical or natural association between two or more things." An even better one is the second one listed: "A connection of people by blood or marriage: kinship." Many times we say we are in a relationship with someone. If we're not married, according to the above definition, then we really aren't in a relationship. However, when two people are married, it always seems like if they decide to get divorced, there are so many roadblocks put up to make the process harder. This may be a good thing. The divorce process being as tedious as it is, may have saved many families from breaking apart during a difficult period that would eventually pass.

"...And a Man is valued by what others say of him."

-from Proverbs 27:21-

Question #1: **Do you know what kind of relationship you are looking for? Do you feel you're marriage material?** I cannot say this enough. Please get a definite answer when you ask a man this first question. It has already been asked in a different way in an earlier part of the book. Try and ask the above questions at two totally different times. This chapter should probably be the first one! Don't try and change a man if he isn't looking to be in the same type of relationship as you.

There is someone out there that is looking for the same thing. Just know that if he tells you he is only looking for friends, don't assume that you know what his definition of a friend is. Ask him what his definition of a friend is. If you are only looking to be just friends let him know. However, be honest with yourself. Telling a man that you are looking to be friends that may develop into something later may be walking a tight rope. You may be causing thoughts to appear in your mind and his, that may cause things to move a little too quickly. If you both decide to become serious at a later date, discuss this further before "relations" enter the relationship.

Question #2: Are you afraid of commitment? *If not, why aren't you already married, engaged to become married, or courting?* I've heard guys say, "If a woman is not married, has never been married, wants to be married, has no children, and is well over the age of 30, something must be wrong with her." I am not saying she isn't a good choice for someone. I'm not saying that she has not been engaged. I am not even saying she wouldn't make a good wife, but there may be something there that she is not willing to reveal to you. The same thing applies to men. Some men play with women's mind with the idea of getting married. They know just what to do to keep you there. By asking this question, you should be able to spot these type of men quickly. The new thing seems to be women wanting to wait until they get done with their education, they have a great guy that they love, but wants him to wait until she is established on her own.

By this time, the woman is in her late 20's may be still dating this same guy from 3,4,5 years ago, wants to be married now, but this guy looks at this time in his life now as "Open Season." While she was getting herself established, he was also getting himself established. Now, since he understands that he is a commodity, he doesn't see the importance of getting married and desires to stay a bachelor just a little while longer. I was talking to a nice hard-working attractive young lady that was about 25. She told me about an attractive and financially successful, 40-year old man she was seeing. He was single, never married, has a child by another woman, says he wants to get married, but hasn't found the right woman. LOL I just laughed. I am not one to judge. However, I felt kind of bad because I was telling her about the book and she asked me, "What should I do?" I laughed more. She knew what she needed to do. Next question please.

Question #3: **What happened with your last relationship that caused it to end?** This is something that you need to know. When it comes to relationships, people have the tendency to do what they did in a previous relationship. If a man beat his last wife, he may have the tendency to do the same with the next. If he massaged the last wife's feet 2 or 3 times a week, he may have the tendency to do the same with the next. Anyway, the answer to this question is another one of those that should let you know if he blames everything on her, or can he take some of the responsibility for what went wrong. One of my Uncle's has been married three times. He felt very bad after the first two marriages didn't work. I remember him trying to figure out what he may have done wrong or could have done differently. The more you know; the better off you may be when it comes to making a good choice.

Question #4: **What is the longest time you have been committed and faithful to one woman?** This is something that you may or may not want to know. If a man tells you six months, he hasn't been committed, or that he has been with 4 women and the longest period of time was 5 or 6 months, you may need to move around. If he says a year, you may need to move around. You should be able to tell from this answer if he is even thinking about a serious relationship. This goes back to what I said earlier in the book, *"Every man is not marriage material."* You just have to understand that and accept that. Some men just don't desire to be faithful or want to get married.

Question #5: **How long have you been friends with the current group of friends?** A man that has friends from childhood, high school, or college that he is still involved with, may have the desire to keep the woman he desires for a long time as well. There was this poem I read many years ago about friends. In the poem, one line said, "Get new friends, but keep the old ones." Old friends say much about you. They know you well and have dealt with you for many years. Many times you have been there for them through family deaths, marriage break ups, their first child, high school and college graduation, fights, sickness, and who knows what else.

"The righteous should choose his friends carefully,
For the way of the wicked leads them astray."

-Proverbs 12:26-

Question #6: **What qualities do you feel it takes to have a successful marriage? Do you feel you possess these qualities?** In Chapter 12, Question #7, I spoke of asking a man, *"Do you see yourself starting your own family? How do you feel about one day starting your own family?* These particular questions may go hand-in-hand. If a man tells you "YES!" to question #7 in chapter 12, he will have thought about what it takes to be a part of a successful marriage. If he wasn't honest when he answered either of the questions, the two answers may have no re-semblance to each other. One of the main answers that I have received most from both men and women is HONESTY. The other is TRUST. There are many qualities that one must possess in order to have any successful rela-tionship. Above all honesty is probably the most important. This leads me to the next question.

List 9 qualities you feel you must possess to have a success-ful marriage:

1.)_____ 2.)_____ 3.)_____

4.)_____ 5.)_____ 6.)_____

7.)_____ 8.)_____ 9.)_____

Question #7: Have you ever broken the trust in a relationship? In some way, knowingly and/or unknowingly most people have done something that has violated the trust in a relationship. Thank God for mercy. Many times throughout the Koran and the Bible, it speaks of the mercy of the Creator. When the trust is broken in a relationship, it causes doubt. Faith and doubt can't exist in the same space at the same time. If a person has broken the trust, it breaks down the confidence in the relationship. Once this becomes continual, it is hard to break that kind of habit. Breaking the trust isn't have to only having sex with another person. Breaking the trust also deals with saying you are going to do something and you don't do it. When this happens over and over again, almost all trust in the relationship can be lost. We should all strive to make our word our bond. Sometimes there are certain things that we have no control over, but most of the time, we can and should strive harder to keep our word. Listen to the man, and then watch his actions to see how much he doesn't do what he says he is going to do.

Question #8: Have you ever been married? If he has been married ask him, **"Are you divorced or separated?"** This is an interesting question if the man has been married because you don't know what you are going to get from it. A man can tell you, "I was married, but we aren't together anymore." As a woman, you may be like, "Oh okay, sorry to hear that. What happened?" He will probably tell you what happened, but what he may not tell you is that they are only "Separated." He may also tell you that they are going through a divorce. If the divorce isn't final, their relationship by law and by the laws of God isn't over.

Therefore, pull back and pull away for your own safety, respect of the other woman, and for your own virtue. It is not wise at all to get involved with a married man. Especially if you know he is married.

Question #9: **What is your relationship like with the Creator of the Heavens and the Earth, God, Allah, Yahweh, Jehovah, I Am, etc.? ...**The 99th Question.

I don't even know where to begin when it comes to the importance of this question. I will begin with this...In the 31st chapter 14th and 15th verse of the Koran it reads; 14) "We have enjoined on man concerning his parents – his mother bears him with faintings upon faintings and his weaning takes two years – saying: Give thanks to Me and to thy parents. To Me is the eventual coming. 15) And if they strive with thee to make thee associate with Me that of which thou has no knowledge, obey them not, and keep kindly company with them in this world, and follow the way of him who turns to Me; then to Me is your return, then I shall inform you of what you did."

From reading these two verses many times in college, I realized that my relationship with my parents was very important. I also realized that my relationship with the source from where both they and I originated, was of the most importance. In the Bible, in the book of Job, Job was put through a serious test. In the book of Job 2:9-10, read what went on, and try to hear his wife's voice and picture both of their faces in your mind by the words she says.

And it reads, *9) Then his wife said to him, "Do you still hold fast to your integrity? Curse God and die!" 10) But he said to her, "You speak as one of the foolish women speaks. Shall we indeed accept good from God, and shall we not accept adversity?" In all this Job did not sin with his lips.*

Even Job's wife couldn't shake his faith and relationship he had with his Creator. For that, if you read the rest of the book of Job, Allah (God) blessed him with more than he previously had, and extended his life to 120 years. In the book of Daniel, another picture of men that kept their faith in Jehovah is the story of Daniel, Shadrach, Meshach, and Abed-Nego. Because of their relationship with the God of Heaven, they were all delivered from serious trials. Read the story. If you've never read the book of Daniel, please take some time to read it. You can also read the 31st Chapter of the Koran. They have both helped remind me in some very tough times, that The Supreme Being would see me through. You must know how his relationship is with the Creator.

Chapter 14
9 Questions you must ask Yourself

The most important chapter of the book just may be this chapter. Telling yourself the truth and being able to be honest to yourself is very important. Being able to get along with yourself and improve who you are as an individual could possibly be one of the most important components to having a successful relationship. Learning to really love yourself is another key to being able to love a man. As a woman, you are the key. You have been blessed with being able to bring new life into existence. As men, we can't do that. We contribute our part in this process, but we can't hold the future in our physical womb because we don't have one. You as a woman, female, lady, or however you see yourself are a divine BLESSING from the Creator.

"A nation can rise no higher than its woman."

-Minister Louis Farrakhan-

Question #1: **What type of relationship do I really desire?** This question and the other questions that follow, are questions you need to know and answer before moving forward with a man. More and more women are saying that they want to be single. This may be true for a few, but I have talked to many women that have admitted to me that really in truly they want a man to be married. Making a real decision that you want a certain kind of relationship, will get you the kind of relationship you desire. Remember...
"Two are better than one."

The kind of man that you truly desire, is the kind that you will attract. You attract what you want into your life. Understand that the kind of woman you are will more than likely attract a certain kind of man. Know what type of relationship you desire for your life.

Question #2: **Am I willing to be the woman that the creator has for me to be? Do I even know what kind of woman he desires for me to be?** These are "YES!" and/or "NO!" questions. Either you are willing to become the type of woman that God desires for you to be or either you aren't. Let me give you just a little bit more of what his word says concerning this from both the Bible and the Koran. In the 4th chapter of the Koran, and in the middle of the 34th verse it reads: "So the good women are obedient, guarding the unseen as Allah has guarded." In this section of the Koran, it is said to mean "obedient to Allah (God)." Therefore your obedience to God comes first. Guarding the unseen means; guarding that which God has given you to be shared with your husband, or being chaste. In the book of Peter chapter 3 verses 1-4, it reads: "Wives likewise, be submissive to your own husbands, that even if some do not obey the word, they, without a word, may be won by the conduct of their wives. 2) When they observe your chaste conduct accompanied by fear. 3) Do not let your adornment be merely outward – arranging the hair, wearing, gold or putting on fine apparel- 4) rather let it be the hidden person of the heart, with the *incorruptible beauty* of a gentle and quiet spirit, which is very precious in the sight of God." The inside is what God is concerned most with.

If the inside is in order, the outside has no choice but to be in order. He is concerned with your heart, and your spirit, and you fearing him. Incorruptible, according to the American Heritage Dictionary, Third Edition, means: "1.) Incapable of being morally corrupted. 2.) Not subject to decay." The book of Proverbs finishes with these words, 31:30 reads; *"Charm is deceitful and beauty is passing, But a woman who fears the Lord, she shall be praised."* The beauty of a woman is her inner beauty. Your physical beauty will one day fade away. What can't be replaced is the incorruptible beauty of her gentle and quiet spirit. The Bible says that this is what is precious in the sight of God. In a world where the outside appearance is the main thing we focus upon, we sometimes forget about what God is most concerned about. Choose to be precious in the sight of God.

Question #3: **What is a virtuous woman? Do I have the qualities of a virtuous woman or the potential to become a virtuous woman, or do I desire to be a contentious woman, a harlot, seductress, or an immoral woman?** Let's go straight to the Bible again. In Proverbs, 11:16 it begins by saying, "A gracious woman retains honor." One thing I have learned about dealing with people is that they sometimes think you are judging them when you say certain things. Again, I am not judging anyone. I am only concerned about the future of our nation and our world, which I know is in the womb of the mind, the woman. Especially the generation I am apart of. They call us generation "Y."

As stated earlier, "A nation can rise no higher than its woman." You can tell the condition of a people by looking at its women. A beautiful picture is painted of the kind of woman that I feel can change the world. In the 31st chapter of proverbs beginning with the 10th verse to the 31st verse, the picture of the virtuous woman is painted. It asks a question... *"Who can find a virtuous wife?"* I will let you get your Bible for yourself and read. I will however, point out a few things that caught my attention about the virtuous woman.

1. She worked. Not only did she work, but she <u>willingly worked</u>.

2. She brought the best food for her and her household. Not some fast food, TV dinner, take out, or delivery.

3. She got up early in the morning before the sun came up to provide a good meal for her family.

4. She seemed to know how to run the household finances & her husband safely trusted her.

5. She exercised! Yes, she exercised.

6. She helped the poor and needy.

7. She was not concerned about lack in her own household.

8. Everyone in her house wore quality clothing.

9. She could sew.

10. She dressed with class.

11. She was obviously respected because her husband was known by the elder members in his society.
12. She spoke with wisdom when she spoke, and not with a foul mouth.
13. The part I love the most is verse 29, it reads; "She watches over the ways of her household, and **does not eat the bread of idleness."** If she was in today's society, she wouldn't be type of woman that watched TV all day and night, was on the phone all the time gossiping and talking bad about people, or spent hours all the time doing nothing productive for herself or anyone else.
14. On top of all this, she feared the Lord.

This type of woman is said to be worth much more than rubies. Rubies are a very precious and valuable stone. Go to a jeweler and see how much rubies are worth. This type of woman is the type of woman that a man doesn't want to get rid of. On the other hand, the book of Proverbs also speaks about two other types of women, a contentious woman and a harlot. Let's first get the definition of both from the 3rd Edition of the American Heritage Dictionary. The word contentious means "Quarrelsome." A synonym for the word contentious is "argumentative." Harlot means: 1) A prostitute. 2) Vagabond. So let's go to the book of Proverbs, chapter 7. I will let you read the whole chapter for yourself. I don't want to put the whole chapter here for you, but I do want to make a point. It's 27 verses that are very important. Once again, in this particular chapter of the book of Proverbs it begins with someone giving advice and wisdom to a young man. In this chapter it warns him of the *immoral* woman, and the seductress who flatters with her lips. It tells about a woman that was married, and while her husband was gone…You know what…I am going to go ahead and put a large portion of the chapter here for you because I want to make sure you read it. Beginning with verse 6 in the 7th chapter of the book of Proverbs, it reads:

> *For at the window of my house I looked through my lattice,*
> *And saw among the simple, I perceived among the youths, a young man devoid of understanding,*
> *Passing along the street near her corner; And he took the path near her house*
> *In the twilight, in the evening, in the black and dark night.*
> *And there a woman met him, with the attire of a HARLOT, and a crafty heart.*
> *She was loud and rebellious, Her feet would not stay at home.*
> *At times she was outside, at times in the open square, lurking at every corner.*
> *So she caught him and kissed him; With an impudent face she said to him:*
> *I have peace offerings with me; Today I have paid my vows.*
> *So I came out to meet you, Diligently to seek your face,*

and I have found you.

I have spread my bed with tapestry, colored coverings of Egyptian linen.

I have perfumed my bed with myrrh, aloes, and cinnamon.

Come let us take our fill of love until the morning; Let us delight ourselves with love.

For my husband is not at home; He has gone on a long journey;

He has taken a bag of money with him, and will come home on the appointed day."

With her enticing speech she caused him to yield, With her flattering lips she seduced him.

Immediately he went after her, as an ox goes to the slaughter, Or as a fool to the correction of the stocks, Till an arrow struck his liver. As a bird hastens to the snare,

He did not know it would cost his life.

Now therefore, listen to me, my children; Pay attention to the words of my mouth:

Do not let your heart turn aside to her ways, Do not stray into her paths;

For she has cast down many wounded, And all who were slain were strong men.

Her house is the way to hell, descending to the chambers of death.

Proverbs has many other verses stating the type of woman to be and not to be.

6:23-26 — For the commandment is a lamp, and the law a light; Reproofs of instruction are the way of life, to keep you from the evil woman, From the flattering tongue of a seductress. Do not lust after her beauty in your heart, nor let her allure you with her eyelids. ***For by means of a harlot a man is reduced to a crust of bread.***

11:22 — As a ring of gold in a swine's snout, So is a lovely woman who lacks discretion.

12:4 — An excellent wife is the crown of her husband, But she who causes shame is like rottenness to his bones.

14:1 — The wise woman builds her house, but the foolish woman pulls it down with her hands.

19:13 - ..."And the contentions of a wife are a continual drip."

19:14 — Houses and riches are an inheritance from fathers, but a prudent wife is from the Lord.

22:14 — The mouth of the immoral woman is a deep pit; He who is abhorred by the Lord will fall there.

23:26-28 — My son, give me your heart, and let your eyes observe my ways. For a harlot is a deep pit, and a seductress is a narrow well. She also lies in wait as for a victim, and increases the unfaithful among men.

27:15 – A continual dripping on a very rainy day and a

contentious woman are alike.

The following story in the Koran speaks about Joseph resisting temptation:

<u>Holy Koran Chapter 12 verses 22-29</u>
And when he attained his maturity, We gave him wisdom and knowledge. And thus do We reward the doers of good.
And she in whose house he was, sought to seduce him, and made fast the doors and said: Come. He said: Allah forbid! Surely my Lord made good my abode. The wrongdoers never prosper.
And certainly she desired him, and he would have desired her, were it not that he had seen the manifest evidence of his Lord. Thus (it as) that We might turn away from him evil and indecency. Surely he was one of Our chosen servants.
And they raced with one another to the door, and she rent his shirt from behind, and they met her husband at the door. She said: What is the punishment for one who intends evil to thy wife, except imprisonment or a painful chastisement?
He said: She sought to seduce me. And a witness of her own family bore witness: If his shirt is rent (ripped) in the front, she speaks the truth and he is of the liars.
And if his shirt is rent behind, she tells a lie and he is of the truthful.
So, when he saw his shirt rent behind, he said: Surely it is a device of you women. Your device is indeed great!
O Joseph, turn aside from this. And (O my wife), ask forgiveness for thy sin. Surely thou art one of the sinful.

As a woman, you really are the key. The above words are only a small piece of the Bible and an even smaller piece of the Koran. However, throughout both of these revealed words from his servants, you are the key. Which woman will you choose to be?

Question #4: What can I do to improve my current financial situation? If you are a woman looking to be with a man with money, you may need to be a woman with money. Even if you are a woman with money, there is some way you can improve your current financial situation. Find out what you desire, why you desire it, and then go for it There is nothing wrong with seeking counsel from people that have been where you are trying to go. Proverbs 15:22 reads: "Without counsel, plans go awry. But in the multitude of counselors they are established." For some reason many young ladies I know and have met don't seem to attach themselves with older female mentors. This would be a good thing to do. Proverbs 16:16 reads: "How much better to get wisdom than gold! And to get understanding is to be chosen than rather silver." To the ladies reading this book that are a little more mature, help mentor some young lady. If you do decide to mentor a young lady, please do so out of love. Understand that our generation is a little different than yours, but there are still timeless jewels that you can share. Lastly, to the young ladies reading this, know that the Virtuous woman worked. If you are a young lady that is healthy, and you're not in school, why not work? I sometimes hear females speak of getting married to someone rich, and staying home all day while doing nothing productive.

Again, you are the KEY! A man could lose it all, so why not work? "Two are better than one." Two incomes are better than one. If he falls, you can pick him up!

Question #5: **How can I improve my education?** The best way to improve your education is to read. If you can't afford a class, pick up a book on a read it. Read it as if you have to teach it to someone. You'll be amazed how much you will learn. The knowledge you gain may one day be needed outside your current profession.

Question #6: **Emotionally, what can I do to improve myself to be able to have a Great relationship with a man that desires the same?** Emotional hurt from the past has in some way or another affected us all. Ninety percent (90%) of what happens to us is how we respond to it, and the other ten percent (10%) is actually what happened. Professional help and spiritual counsel have helped many people.

I have a story about a famous woman. She's an absolutely gorgeous woman to me. I had the opportunity to meet her while working at Victoria's Secret, She was raped when she was working one night before she became famous. In a magazine interview she expressed how she made it through this devastating situation. The interesting part to me was that she didn't let it take away her whole life. Although it has probably had a negative effect on her relationships with men, she didn't let that one event define who she was. I seriously knew at that point that you can't judge an individual because you don't know what they've been through. When I met her in Victoria's Secret, I knew at that point why she was famous.

She had this radiance around her that was unmistakable. She had no make up on, a jogging suit, and was very non-assuming. However, her spirit kind of reached out and grabbed even the individuals that didn't know who she was. Try your best to rise above negative emotions.

Question #7: What can I do to improve my health? Most of you know the answer to this. The first thing to do is get a physical examination. From there, begin to think healthy thoughts. Speak healthy words. The Bible says, "Death and life are in the power of the tongue..." Therefore, if you want to be healthier begin to say, "I am healthier." When you do this, you give your body the power to become healthier. If you are sick, don't say, "I am sick." The more you say it, the more real your sickness becomes. In the 31st Chapter of the Koran, it says in verse 20, "See you not that Allah has made subservient to you whatever is in the heavens and whatever is in the earth, and granted to you His favors complete outwardly and inwardly?" Everything including your health is subservient to you. Your health is to help you navigate through life to be able to have that which you desire. It is hard to enjoy anything in bad health. If you need to lose weight, exercise more, see a dentist, start flossing, start eating better, or anything else to improve your health, just do it! You have to know that in today's society, information is everywhere. In many magazines there always seems to be something about improving your health. I don't think the magazines would publish these articles if they didn't work.

Educate yourself on becoming healthier, and then take the necessary action to do so. "If not now...when? If not you...then who?"

Question #8: **Have I defined what happiness is for me?** An individual has to decide they are going to be a happy individual regardless. In India Arie's song, "There's Hope," I feel that she expresses this. We sometimes have the tendency to think that money, material possessions, and other people make us happy. All these things contribute to our overall happiness, but unless we are happy with ourselves we can never really in truly be happy. In another speech I heard by Zig Ziglar, he said, "Happiness is not pleasure. Happiness is victory!" When I saw the movie, "Pursuit of Happyness," I actually cried. It was probably the first movie that I've ever cried about. It was an uncontrollable cry. I felt that at that point, in Chris Gardner's life he had obtained happiness because he overcame a very tough period, achieved what he set out to do, and was VICTORIOUS! After so much disappointment, he finally had a VICTORY! What is your definition of happiness?

Question #9: **What can I do to improve my relationship with the Creator of me?** Well, well, well. All the questions in the book are questions that you must ask yourself, and the opposite sex. I would say, that there are many things you can do to improve your relationship with the Creator (Allah, Yahweh, God, I Am, Jehovah, etc.). It's a lifelong process.

Just as technology continues to improve, our relationship with the one source from which all things originate can continue to improve. By reading and understanding the Bible, The Koran, Torah, the study of other so-called religions, math, science, history, and definitely yourself, your relationship with the Creator can improve. Just as everything else that is brought into fruition, this starts with a firm decision in your own mind.

In Conclusion

In conclusion, as a young man, I would love to see women loving each other and respecting one another much more. Regardless of your race, religion, ethnic background, social status, language, or national origin, love and respect one another. I would love to see women respecting each other's relationships. I would love to see women respecting their bodies, in every sense of the word. I would love to see women giving more of their time to help others. I would love to see women standing firm beside the educator's in our society because I watched my mother teach for many years and not get much respect and appreciation for a job well done. I would like for women to love each other's differences in personality and understand that each of you need one another. I would like for women to be less catty towards one another and understand that each of you are special. I would love to see less envy towards each other because of a gift that has been given to someone else that you may feel doesn't deserve that gift. I would like for you to work on you, and understand that as the Bible says, "A man's gift will make room for him." I would like for you to know that you are man because your womb is the first place for growth and development of the mind of both male and female. So know that your gift, however great or small you may think it is, will make room for you. Therefore, develop you. Get to know yourself, and in doing so, you will get to know the Creator of the universe. Woman, you are the KEY!

Thank you for taking the time to read this book. I hope and pray that you were blessed in some way from it. May All Mighty God, Yahweh, Allah, Jehovah, I Am, or whatever name you prefer to call him by, continue to bless you, elevate you, and keep you. May his PEACE, be with you always!

Claim the Increase!

Your Brother,

Armani

Armani Valentino